Original title:
The House of Quiet Moments

Copyright © 2025 Creative Arts Management OÜ
All rights reserved.

Author: Thomas Sinclair
ISBN HARDBACK: 978-1-80587-049-4
ISBN PAPERBACK: 978-1-80587-519-2

Sighs of the Sunlight

Sunlight spills like lemonade,
Tickling toes that won't behave.
Laughter dances on the breeze,
As shadows play a game of tease.

Mismatched socks in soft retreat,
Sneaky cats with nimble feet.
A butterfly joins in the fun,
Chasing tails beneath the sun.

Hushed Conversations

Whispers crawl between the walls,
As the kettle softly calls.
Cookies giggle on the shelf,
Mocking us for being ourselves.

Time stands still, but laughs a lot,
While dust bunnies plot a plot.
The clock ticks in a jazzy way,
Making every minute play.

Memories in the Dust

Dust collects like silly tales,
On chairs that creak and never fail.
Old photographs with winking eyes,
Tell stories that tell no lies.

The rug knows every dance we share,
While slippers play a light affair.
A tea cup chuckles on the stand,
Holding secrets from the land.

A Stillness of Time

In the corners, echoes hum,
While the oven keeps a drum.
A nosey squirrel peers inside,
As if to ask where's the ride?

Windows creak with tales of cheer,
While laughter floats from ear to ear.
The teapot smiles, it knows the score,
As we sip and crave for more.

The Pulse of Quietude

In the room where whispers lay,
Chairs dance lightly, come what may.
Dust bunnies plot to take their flight,
Tickling toes in the dead of night.

Inanimate friends host a tea,
With crumpets made of fantasy.
Lampshades giggle without a sound,
As socks and slippers spin around.

Sofa cushions catch a fleeting rhyme,
While clocks play tricks, delaying time.
A curtain's sway, a playful jest,
As silence claims its cozy rest.

Joy wraps the corners, snug and tight,
In silent mayhem, pure delight.
Here, laughter lingers, shy yet bold,
In moments soft, our secrets told.

Harmony in the Hush

Boring moments wear a grin,
As paperclips start to spin.
The cat holds court on a pile of clothes,
While a dust mote wears a funny nose.

A breeze that whistles through the crack,
Sings songs of socks that wander back.
Muffled giggles from the broom,
As it sweeps away the gloom.

Chandeliers hum a nonsense tune,
While shadows dance beneath the moon.
In this calm, a smirk unfurls,
As quiet chaos softly swirls.

Time pauses for a playful sigh,
As laughter twinkles in the eye.
In each still corner, joy ignites,
Transforming silence into flights.

Breath of a New Day

Morning yawns with sleepy grace,
Coffee scents embrace the space.
The cat plots mischief, eyes aglow,
As toast pops up with a cheerful 'hello!'

Sunbeams dance upon the floor,
Socks mismatched near the door.
Laughing at the day's young start,
With giggles bubbling, there's joy to impart.

Fragments of Forgotten Laughter

Echoes of chuckles from the past,
Jokes we've told that never last.
The old chair creaks, a knowing friend,
Whispering secrets that never end.

Spilled tea on the carpet, what a sight!
Laughter erupts, a pure delight.
Photos stuck in awkward poses,
Our faces bloom like silly roses.

Corners of Comfort

A blanket fort that's sagging low,
With snacks tucked in, it's time for a show.
The dog snores softly, dreaming dreams,
While we plot schemes of ice cream extremes.

Pillows tossed like clouds of fluff,
This cozy nook is just enough.
With popcorn flying, a cheerful mess,
Together we laugh, nothing less.

Patterns of Restfulness

Naps are sacred, that's the rule,
Wearing pajamas as a school.
With faces pressed in sleepy grace,
We snooze away, time slows its pace.

The clock ticks softly, what a tease,
As daydreams drift with gentle ease.
In the silliness of cozy times,
Our whispered jokes are priceless rhymes.

The Calm Before the Dawn

In the still of night, a cat snores loud,
Dreaming of fish, while wrapped in a shroud.
Sneaky squirrels tease from the window's view,
And the coffee pot hums, 'Oh, what shall we brew?'

Curtains dance softly, a ghost in the light,
Chasing shadows as dawn takes its flight.
The clock ticks and tocks, making all kinds of sounds,
Laughter in stillness, where joy knows no bounds.

Fleeting Moments of Grace

A slip of the sock, and down goes the cat,
In the race for the sunlight, can you believe that?
Mismatched shoes laughing, they scatter the floor,
As the dog spies a squirrel, and forgets the door.

A clock that ticks backwards, what madness is here?
Time waves hello, then disappears in a cheer.
Bittersweet kisses from the cake on the plate,
A moment of grace, then we all contemplate.

Pattering Raindrops on Roofs

Raindrops are drummers, a band in the night,
The roof is their stage, oh what a sight!
Puddles reflect, oh, a circus of rain,
While boots leap and splatter—let's dance in the lane!

Umbrellas like mushrooms sprout out of the ground,
Each one a giant, they bump and they mound.
Someone slips and giggles, the day turns to play,
And laughter finds ways to chase clouds away.

Hidden Nooks of Reflection

In corners forgotten, a dust bunny reigns,
He guards all the secrets, the laughs and the pains.
A mirror that winks, with a sly little grin,
Says, "Let's celebrate all the nonsense within!"

The sofa's a fortress, where chaos unfolds,
Blankets as capes, for adventures retold.
With popcorn confetti, we dance on delight,
In those hidden nooks, oh, we shine ever bright.

When Stillness Speaks

In the corner, socks do dance,
Whispers of laundry take their chance.
The cat looks on, with wise intent,
Plotting schemes of sweet content.

Ticking clocks try to laugh aloud,
Tickling time, oh silly crowd!
Each second wears a goofy grin,
As the dog rolls over, wild in sin.

Cushions bounce in happy cheer,
They've held more secrets than a seer.
In quiet moments, giggles swell,
Echoes of tales only they can tell.

Lullabies of the Past

Once a shoe sang lullabies,
To a child with sleepy eyes.
Now it rests, with laces tied,
In the shadows, where dreams abide.

Crayons speak in colors bright,
Cartwheeling ghosts in fading light.
Each scribble tells a story clear,
Of monsters that we used to fear.

Beneath the bed, old memories snooze,
Dust bunnies whisper silly blues.
The nightlight flickers, softly jokes,
As teddy bears indulge in pokes.

Hidden Nooks and Crannies

Behind the fridge, the dust bunnies play,
Holding parties at the end of the day.
Cookies left to gather dust,
In secret spots, they gather rust.

In the pantry, whispers fly,
As expired cans begin to sigh.
They share tales of what was once,
Curious flavors now a dunce.

Battered shoes have stories told,
Of adventures brave and bold.
In the corners, laughter drips,
From mishaps, joy forever slips.

The Weight of Unspoken Words

In the air, a joke holds tight,
Waiting for a giggle's flight.
Pillow forts hold whispered dreams,
The rabbit snickers, or so it seems.

Socks with holes just roll their eyes,
Claiming wisdom in disguise.
Each glance exchanged deserves a laugh,
As the broom takes the paper's path.

Stories buried in the floor,
Of midnight snacks, oh what a score!
Secrets hide in every fold,
Of chairs that squeak, both strong and bold.

Fabric of Still Waters

In a corner, a cat takes a nap,
While mice hold a tiny map.
They plan a feast under the table,
Where crumbs are plentiful and fables.

The teapot whistles with strong demands,
Yet the kettle always misunderstands.
It sings a tune too high for tea,
As the scones roll off with glee.

Dust bunnies play hide and seek,
They've mastered the art of mystique.
Each leap a dance, a fluffy flight,
Under the glow of the soft porch light.

A chair squeaks tales of wear and tear,
As if to say, "I was once quite rare."
Now it holds giggles, spills, and dreams,
In the fabric of laughter, nothing's as it seems.

Peace Found in Shadows

In shadows deep, a sock does roam,
It's lost long from its cozy home.
Cats dart across like ninja spies,
As dust motes swirl in sunlit skies.

A cricket chirps a silly song,
The broom sways like it's all gone wrong.
Every corner tells a joke well-kept,
Even the creaky stairs have leapt.

The clock strikes funny, time does flip,
As teacups dance on a charming trip.
Warmth and whimsy go hand in hand,
In this playful, well-worn land.

And so they laugh in whispered tones,
These moments stitched in cozy bones.
Here's to mischief, a soft embrace,
In the shadows, we find our place.

Celestial Dreams in Simplicity

Stars peep through the window frame,
Winking like they're in a game.
A blanket fort forms a little sky,
Where laughter soars and dreams can fly.

A goldfish floats with a silly pose,
While the dog contemplates his woes.
Frog leaps from books with a loud croak,
Shushing the bunny who starts to poke.

Clouds of fluff from the pillows burst,
As giggles spill out, oh what a first!
Each moment counts, each second shines,
In our hearts where the silly entwines.

So here we sit, lost in delight,
Wishing that this night takes flight.
A canvas of chaos, a gentle play,
In celestial simplicity, we sway.

Threads of Gentle Light

Sunbeams peek through an attic door,
Chasing dust bunnies forevermore.
A tape measure stretches its tight grip,
While the old chair takes a silent trip.

Spools of laughter roll on the floor,
As socks gossip, "We've seen it all before!"
Thread needles perform their flawless dance,
Darning dreams in an odd romance.

Time ticks by with a comical sigh,
Reminders of woes with a wink and a pie.
Every stitch holds a tiny tale,
Of misfits and dreams that never pale.

So let the light glow soft and bright,
In our antics, there's pure delight.
With each little moment, we sew and twirl,
In the fabric of life, we giggle and whirl.

The Charm of Stillness

In corners where dust bunnies play,
A hammock sways in a lazy way.
The cat pursues a ghostly sprite,
But naps instead, what a silly sight.

Chairs creak under weight like a song,
When laughter escapes, it's never wrong.
Tea cups chatter, a symphony brewed,
While cookies conspire to break the mood.

Shadows dance in a slow-motion waltz,
Where socks often vanish without assaults.
We giggle at nothing and everything too,
In this calm place, where time feels askew.

A vase holds the secrets of laughter sweet,
As chairs table gossip, a friendly feat.
In stillness we find the joy that's divine,
In moments of silence, the hearts intertwine.

Pools of Tranquil Reflection

Mirrors reflect the silliest frowns,
While rubber ducks wear tiny crowns.
In a bubble bath, the world disappears,
Taking laughter with all our fears.

A goldfish judges from the glass globe,
With a wiggle, it's quite the probe.
Watch the drips from the nose of a clown,
As we ponder on why he might frown.

Cups of cocoa in hand firmly hold,
They share tales of mischief we're told.
Floating along on the rippling side,
In moments of joy, we take pride.

Footsteps echo, a playful dance,
As socks collide in a silly chance.
The laughter lingers, a soft, teasing chat,
In this quiet wonderland, we welcome a pat.

Lighthouses of Solitude

In the glow of a single, soft light,
A lamp spills warmth in the quiet night.
Worn slippers shuffle across the floor,
As the dog snores softly—what's it snoring for?

The kettle whistles a happy tune,
While cookies call like a well-mannered rune.
Jokes told twice land like feathers in air,
Our memories floating with love and care.

Puzzles gather dust in a corner so bold,
But the laughter shared is a treasure gold.
In solitude's grip, we steal a smile,
Shining brightly, though it's just for a while.

A postcard sits, carrying tales of sun,
Implying that solitude can still be fun.
With a wink from a shadow, or giggle in spite,
We find sailing in silence a whimsical flight.

Warmth in Familiar Corners

A corner chair holds tales of the past,
With cushions that fit like a friendly cast.
Beneath a blanket, we snuggle so tight,
While dust motes dance in the golden light.

Old slippers lie in a lazy array,
As our giggles chase the gloom far away.
The clock ticks softly, a perceptive friend,
Measuring moments that never must end.

Recipes whisper from pages worn,
Of laughter and cheer that always adorn.
A teapot sings softly, a note of delight,
As we sip our stories, the world feels right.

Comfy corners wrap us in their embrace,
As laughter rings bright in this sacred space.
In every still moment, we find our bliss,
With the warmest of hugs and a gentle kiss.

Gentle Breaths of Evening

Crisp air whispers secrets low,
While cats chase shadows to and fro,
A chair creaks with a tired sigh,
As socks play hide and seek nearby.

Tea cups dance with giggly flair,
A kettle joins with steamy air,
Lamps flicker like a cheeky grin,
Inviting chaos to creep in.

A clock in the corner tickles time,
While dreams on the ceiling softly climb,
The night is filled with chuckles bright,
As stars play tag through the moonlight.

Mismatched cushions piled up high,
A throne for those who dare to try,
With laughter wrapped in every breath,
Here joy finds life, defying death.

Tapestry of Tranquility

Under quilts of patchwork dreams,
Rubber ducks plot silent schemes,
Old records spin with a wink,
The cat pauses, just to think.

Spatulas dance in the fading light,
As omelets flip with pure delight,
Chairs stacked like a comical tower,
Each tick of the clock brings a new hour.

A worn-out shoe lies in repose,
Plays the role of a garden hose,
Jokes are brewed with every cup,
In this calm, we laugh it up.

Candles giggle with gentle glow,
Mysteries hidden in shadows below,
In this snug nook where silence gleams,
Life unfolds with whimsical dreams.

Lullabies of the Light

Sunlight winks through curtain seams,
Pajamas dance in daylight dreams,
The toast pops up with quite a cheer,
As if it knows the fun is near.

Wobbly tables play a trick,
Adventures stir with every flick,
The fridge hums a quiet song,
To which the spices all belong.

A wayward sock makes a new friend,
With a sock from the last weekend,
Rugged laughter fills the space,
In this haven, find your place.

Projector rolls out cartoons bright,
With popcorn fights into the night,
Where giggles echo and dreams take flight,
The world outside feels just right.

Softness of the Heart

A feather falls with gentle grace,
Landing on a smiling face,
A thumb war breaks out with delight,
As kittens plot a daring flight.

The couch holds secrets, laughter loud,
In cozy corners, we feel proud,
Worn pages turn with little hands,
Exploring far-off fairy lands.

A puzzle waits for pieces lost,
While cuddles come at no real cost,
Whispers swirl like candy floss,
In this place, we find no loss.

Socks parade with mismatched glee,
As sunshine winks, oh so free,
In this warmth where laughter starts,
We treasure moments, soft and arts.

Tranquil Corners Unfold

In corners where the dust bunnies play,
Socks dance in a patchwork ballet.
A cat naps on the window ledge,
While the dog dreams of chasing a hedge.

The fridge hums a sassy old tune,
As veggies plot their escape at noon.
A chair creaks with secrets to share,
While shadows giggle, light as air.

A teacup sits with a knowing grin,
As tea leaves whisper tales of sin.
Mugs clatter, the party's begun,
In this place, laughter weighs a ton.

In the nook where old books reside,
Each spine tells tales, none tried to hide.
As silence wraps like a cozy quilt,
The funny moments are carefully built.

Murmurs of the Unseen

Whispers tickle the corners at night,
Chairs giggle, they get such delight.
Ghosts of pizza crust linger on floors,
As leftovers dance right out the doors.

The clock chimes but it is offbeat,
As shadows shuffle on tiny, soft feet.
A broom takes a break, lazy as can be,
While dust dreams of being free like the sea.

Pillows throw a party so grand,
And the blanket brigade takes a stand.
Laughter echoes from walls once gray,
As cozy chaos steals the day.

Here the unseen finds a sweet voice,
In moody tones, they rejoice.
Every creak and every sigh,
Turns a quiet moment awry.

Reflections in a Dusty Frame

In frames where dust gathers like friends,
Memories tease and play pranks that never end.
A flower pot laughs, too shy to speak,
But its soil's tickled, cheek to cheek.

The spoons in the drawer barter for tales,
While forks boast of their spaghetti trails.
Each time the door swings, it brings a cheer,
Echoes of laughter reappear.

A quirk of fate left the light on,
Chasing shadows till they've all gone.
Reflections dance with a wink and a grin,
Making fun of the day that's been.

The cobwebs spin stories of old,
Of mischievous spirits, brave and bold.
In the quiet, it knows how to play,
Turning mundane doubts to a silly ballet.

Soft Footsteps on Worn Floors

Footsteps whisper like secrets shared,
Old stairs chuckle, they've always cared.
A creaky board plays the jester's role,
Announcing the traveler's playful stroll.

The rug claims its spots with a thump,
While old shoes plot a tiny jump.
Muffled giggles hide 'neath the beams,
As curtain folds unveil the dreams.

Clattering cups make a ruckus so fine,
As energy flows like a bold red wine.
The shadows play peek-a-boo, so sly,
Conspiring with laughter that can't help but fly.

The floors rumble, a half-hearted roar,
Worn down but still up for more.
In every step, a story to tell,
Of quiet chuckles that sit well.

Dust Motions in Sunbeams

Dust bunnies dance in lazy light,
Their graceful twirls, a charming sight.
Each particle leaps with cheeky cheer,
Waltzing in sunbeams, winter's veneer.

They spin tales of forgotten lore,
Of mischief on the dusty floor.
As I peek around, they freeze and wait,
With giggles behind the cupboard's gate.

A broom swoops in, they scatter fast,
But next time I'll catch them, I'll hold them fast.
Behind my couch, they plot and scheme,
In a world where dust bunnies reign supreme.

So here's to moments in the dust,
Where giggles linger, and we must trust.
For life's small laughs are more than gold,
In bright sunbeams, their stories unfold.

Unraveled Threads of Thought

In my pocket, a string unwinds,
A tangled mess of daily grinds.
My thoughts roll out like yarn in spring,
A jumbled patchwork, what will it bring?

One thread points to socks, mismatched pairs,
Poking fun at my fashion cares.
Another leads to chocolate bites,
Sweet chaos hiding on sleepless nights.

With each new twist, a laugh erupts,
What's that smell? Oh, it's still in cups!
Forgotten coffee, a morning treat,
Bringing giggles when life feels obsolete.

So I follow along this silly trail,
With joy as my guide, I shall not fail.
For laughter's a thread that never frays,
Weaving through time in whimsical ways.

Calm Beyond the Doorway

A squeaky door leads to calm,
Where moments breathe, and life is balm.
Cushions invite with soft embrace,
I hop across like a silly race.

Inside, the clock ticks at its own pace,
As cats lounge lazily, strutting grace.
A silent realm of quiet smiles,
Where laughter loiters in hidden styles.

But if you tiptoe, beware the cat,
A swish of the tail, then a playful spat.
With a pounce that disrupts my peace,
I laugh as our tussles never cease.

In here the world can fade away,
Where silly thoughts hold sway and play.
Hidden calm lies, like candy in jars,
Welcoming all with a streak of stars.

Portraits of Abandonment

Old chairs sit, painted in dust,
Wondering who, or what, to trust.
A canvas of stories lost and grim,
But their whispers echo, full of whim.

Walls lean in, secrets they share,
Of loud parties or strange affairs.
The portraits hang, just out of view,
With eyes that twinkle like morning dew.

In corners, shoes lie side by side,
With tales of mischief, laughter, and pride.
An abandoned sock spins with delight,
Shining brightly in the fading light.

So here's to places long forgotten,
Where giggles linger and moods lighten.
In portraits where the past feels bright,
Abandonment turns to sheer delight.

Moments Captured in Time

A clock that spins the wrong way,
Ticking notes on a game of play.
Cats in hats do dance and prance,
While goldfish partake in a trance.

Pillows speak in whispers loud,
Making jokes that draw a crowd.
Chairs that wobble, laugh and sway,
Breathe in and out, it's time to play.

Still Water Under a Starlit Sky

In shadows deep, the stars do wink,
While frogs share secrets as they blink.
A fish in bowler hat swims by,
Exchanging glances with the sky.

Mice in tuxedos dance on logs,
To the tune of merry dogs.
A chilly breeze whispers delight,
As crickets chirp through the night.

Gentle Hues of Afternoon

Sunbeams spill in golden rays,
Where toast and jam have fun-filled days.
A squirrel with a monocle stares,
While ants debate in tiny lairs.

Teacups giggle, cakes take flight,
With eager forks in a playful fight.
Butterflies wear colors so bright,
They flirt with breezes, pure delight.

The Lull of an Empty Room

In corners where the dust bunnies play,
A sock and shoe run away from a stray.
Walls are echoing giggles from ages,
Where chairs make up stories like old sages.

A ghost in pajamas floats lazily,
While shadows perform in a spree.
With laughter trapped in every nook,
It's a space where joy gladly took.

Silhouettes of Solitude

In corners dim, the shadows play,
They dance around, then run away.
A cup of tea, a biscuit crumbles,
While laughter in the silence rumbles.

The cat's disdain, a regal pose,
Its judgment felt, as garden grows.
With every tick of clocks that tease,
A moment's pause, a sigh with ease.

I trip on dreams that float and sway,
A sock elusive in the fray.
The chair's embrace, it holds me tight,
As whispers ride the waves of light.

In echoes soft, the silliness,
Prevails in tune with nothingness.
A wigged-out plant with sticky notes,
Hums protocols it never wrote.

Secrets in the Silence

In stillness wrapped, a secret brews,
The cupboard sighs, a ghostly muse.
A sock's escape, a chase unfolds,
As silence spills the truths untold.

The fridge hums softly, tales abound,
Of midnight snacks yet to be found.
The floorboards creak, they hold their breath,
Each moment dull, yet so adept.

The tumbleweed of cotton swabs,
They scatter dreams and endless sobs.
With whims and giggles, off they fly,
Creating mischief, oh my my!

So let's embrace the pause we share,
With playful whispers in the air.
An orchestra of silent cheer,
As laughter drifts, forever near.

Reverie in the Corner

A teacup's rim, a crooked grin,
In quiet realms where dreams begin.
The corners hold forgotten quests,
Where napping cats wear fuzzy vests.

A picture frame, askew with pride,
Echoes how the time slipped by.
The dust motes dance in golden rays,
Chasing thoughts through lazy days.

A clock with hands that tease the hours,
Plays hide and seek amid the flowers.
As stillness wraps like a cozy quilt,
In reverie, my world is built.

A wish upon the ceiling's beam,
A ticklish thought, a gentle dream.
With chuckles bloom in playful light,
The corner cradles joy, so bright.

Timeless Reflections

In mirrored glass, the whims behold,
Reflections whisper tales of old.
An expression, cheeky and spry,
Reads like a joke in passing by.

The moments freeze, a snapshot caught,
Where silly faces swirl thoughts fraught.
With giggles caught like fireflies,
Oh who knew laughter wears disguise?

The clock without a lid, it ticks,
In shades of mischief, playful tricks.
Serendipity, in time's embrace,
Dances lightly to a happy place.

Let's raise a glass to timeless fun,
With echoes rich, the day is won.
In quiet nooks, the laughter rings,
A symphony of little things.

Whispers in the Corner

In the corners, cats conspire,
Plotting mischief, never tired.
Dust bunnies dance with glee,
While socks play hide and seek, you see!

The clock ticks loud, it grumbles twice,
Telling tales of spilled cold rice.
Mirrors giggle, reflecting me,
"Don't trip over that, you silly bee!"

A chair squeaks out a silly joke,
"Why'd the broomstick cross the smoke?"
The curtains snicker, swaying slow,
While I just sit here, stealing the show!

In this home of silly dreams,
Where everything's not as it seems.
Oh, to laugh at every quirk,
Where laughter winks and play's the work!

Echoes of Solitude

Echoes bounce off empty walls,
That sometimes whisper silly calls.
A tea cup giggles, sharing tea,
"Remember me from 2003?"

A shoe once danced all on its own,
Stepping lightly, like a tone.
It left to find its better half,
But now it's just a foot's good laugh!

The spoons conspire in silent chat,
"Which one stirred the coffee brat?"
While the fridge hums a woozy tune,
As if it's serenading the moon.

In solitude's funny embrace,
I find comfort, joy, and grace.
Each echo plays a jest or two,
In this dance of oddities we pursue!

Sunlight through Draped Windows

Sunlight slips through worn-out drapes,
Illuminating cat-shaped shapes.
On cushions bright, they start to prance,
In a yoga class of feline chance!

Dust motes swirl in golden beams,
Like tiny fairies in bright dreams.
The chair's a throne for royal naps,
As laughter tumbles from its laps.

Outside, squirrels plot a heist,
While I sip tea and munch on sliced.
"Who stole my sandwich?" echoes again,
As if my lunch has joined the fun train!

With sunlight dappling the floor,
Every shadow tells a lore.
In comedy, we all can bask,
In the light of life's silly mask!

Shadows of Stillness

Shadows linger, leaning low,
Making faces, putting on shows.
A ghost in slippers wobbles near,
"Watch your step; I'm still right here!"

The clock stands still, hands frozen tight,
Every tick's a tiny fright.
"Must I remind you to unwind?"
It croaks with a sarcastic mind.

A picture frame gossips, it seems,
"Remember that time with the whipped cream?"
While the rug snores a shaggy tune,
As I marvel at its furry swoon.

In stillness where the laughter meets,
Every shadow takes its seats.
Life's comedy plays on this stage,
Where joke and jests greet every age!

Candles Flicker Softly

In the corner, dust bunnies roam,
Chasing shadows, they find their home.
The cat yawns wide, on the sill so high,
Plotting a pounce, oh my, oh my!

Candles drip wax in a subtle dance,
The ghosts of old thoughts take a chance.
They tickle the air with a giddy glow,
Whispers of laughter from long ago.

A clock ticks loud, marking time like a joke,
Each tick a punchline, a rhythmic poke.
Worn-out chairs creak, join in the fun,
Squeaks serenade until day is done.

In this cozy chaos, we gather near,
Sharing secrets only we can hear.
Toasting to moments that make us grin,
On the edge of silliness, let the night begin!

Murmured Dreams at Dusk

The fish in the bowl, they watch, they stare,
As clouds in the sky begin to tear.
Stars pop like popcorn, audibly bright,
Cracking jokes as the sun takes flight.

In the garden, owls hoot with glee,
Trading tales over a cup of tea.
The glow of twilight, a mischievous shade,
Makes every shadow seem over-played.

Laughter spills over like spilled milk,
As crickets chirp in their suits of silk.
The moon nods off, half-sleepy and sly,
Not wanting to miss the evening's high.

Retreating indoors, we giggle and chat,
Hatching plans with a click of the cat.
In these murmurs, we find the light,
Turning simple moments into pure delight!

Edges of a Quiet Mind

Thoughts drift like leaves on a summer breeze,
Swirling around, just as they please.
A chair squeaks softly, it wants to play,
Joining the chatter of another day.

Jars filled with candy, a colorful sight,
Prompt memories sparkling, bright in the night.
Conversations that wobble, giggle, and spin,
Each quirk a treasure, soft grins to win.

The fridge hums tunes like an old jukebox,
Bopping along with its pickle and socks.
Every corner of laughter, we begin to see,
The edges of silence buzz gleefully.

As pillows engage in a friendly debate,
Which one is fluffier? Let's contemplate!
The quiet stretches, stifling a cough,
Together we chuckle, then let it all off!

The Melodic Rustle of Pages

Books stacked high, they whisper and grunt,
Jokesters of wisdom, that's what they want.
With each gentle flip, they're itching to share,
Laughs hidden tightly in layers of air.

The pen squeaks softly, a comedic squawk,
Trying to keep up with the stories they talk.
A puddle of ink forms a happy face,
As paper drifts, joining in on the chase.

Outside, a dog barks an old tune of cheer,
While crickets co-write with uninhibited fear.
The sunlight kicks back with a fizzy sip,
A bubbling laugh from its sunny quip.

Moments swirl like a well-worn quilt,
Stitched with smiles, woven with guilt.
Between the covers, adventures ignite,
In the rustle of pages, humor takes flight!

Unseen Threads of Peace

In corners where dust bunnies sway,
A cat strikes a pose, judging the day.
Socks left behind, a mismatched parade,
Who knew chaos could feel like a trade?

Tea cups are stacked like towers of fun,
Each sip a giggle, each laugh just begun.
Whispers of secrets between the walls,
As time takes its stroll and quietly sprawls.

The clock ticks slowly, or so it seems,
Caught in a haze of whimsical dreams.
Footprints of laughter on tiles of gray,
It's a dance party—just a step away!

Rugged but snug, we nestle and grin,
Life's simplest joys have a way to begin.
With tattered old books and a comfy chair,
Find humor in silence, a laugh in the air.

A Sanctuary of Serenity

In the corner, a chair holds its breath,
You'd swear it's plotting some clever theft.
Socks on the floor, a wiggle and twist,
What's that odor? Oh wait, it's the mist!

A kettle's whistle sings opera at noon,
While memories dance like a cheeky raccoon.
Candles that flicker, but play hide and seek,
"Is that a laugh?"—pot's starting to leak!

Baskets of laundry stack up like dreams,
Every misplaced shirt, a story that beams.
Jokes of mishaps linger in every space,
In this gentle chaos, we all find our place.

The cat plays the piano with paws of delight,
Notes falling softly like feathers in flight.
Embrace the mess, it's a symphony true,
A sanctuary thrives when we dance silly too!

In the Embrace of Silence

Here in the quiet, the crickets conspire,
To map out a maze of laughter and fire.
A blender's hum joins in for a while,
As muffins rise high, bearing pastry style.

Dust motes spin tales of forgotten delight,
Of pranks played by cats in the soft morning light.
With mismatched cushions and slippers askew,
Who knew peace could be just a little askew?

The mailman slips in with a cheeky grin,
He knows every secret we keep tucked within.
Jokes fly like papers in the breeze outside,
In moments of stillness, our joys collide.

A chair creaks its laughter, a table will sway,
And all of the stillness just says, "Let's play!"
In this warm cocoon, we savor the scene,
Where silence brings humor, both gentle and green.

Fleeting Glances of Twilight

As dusk spills its colors, the shadows behave,
A bunny hops past, wearing mischief like a cape.
Laughter echoes softly, sweet as a tune,
Cuz even the stars need a wink from the moon!

A teapot whistles, a kettle sings low,
Leaves tap dance softly, their delicate show.
Windows are open, inviting each breeze,
While socks on the line wave with such ease!

Dishes all piled, a tower of glee,
Each fork has a tale; it's a crockery spree.
Curtains that flutter, embracing the night,
While moments of mirth twinkle with light.

Fleeting and funny, time tiptoes away,
Leaving footprints of joy where our worries would stay.
In quiet reflections where laughter does meet,
Twilight hums softly, keeping hearts sweet.

Cradled in the Glow

In a corner where shadows play,
Laughter bounces in a silly sway,
A cat naps on a chair, snoring loud,
While squirrels plot, feeling quite proud.

Cookies crumble on the floor,
Each bite's a step to smile galore,
Jokes shared over cups of tea,
Marking time with whimsy's spree.

A quilt drapes across old chairs,
Stories linger, float in airs,
With every giggle, warmth unfurls,
Tickling toes and crazy twirls.

As the light begins to fade,
We savor laughter, never weighed,
This whimsy fills the evening's space,
While shadows dance in a silly race.

Moments Wrapped in Warmth

In the kitchen, a kettle sings,
Mismatched cups are fanciful things,
Sugar and cream start a playful fight,
As giggles erupt, what a sight!

The sofa's a ship on stormy seas,
With pillows tossed like swaying trees,
A shipmate's tale bent by jest,
As we navigate this cozy quest.

Whispers of spices linger near,
A recipe's secret, if we'd just hear,
Each stir of the pot brings bubbling cheer,
The warmth of the moment, always near.

Outside, the stars peek through the trees,
While the wind sings softly, with a tease,
Wrapped in laughter, we dwell deep,
In playful moments, love to keep.

Glimmers of Nostalgia

Underneath the old oak tree,
Memories whisper, wild and free,
Each leaf holds stories of days gone by,
With a wink, they flutter, oh my, oh my!

A dance of shadows in the gentle breeze,
Twirling tales that always please,
The past is a canvas splashed with cheer,
Where silly moments linger near.

Crayons scribble on papers bare,
With masterpieces that boldly declare,
A rainbow world where laughter glows,
As we sip juice from curvy hose.

As night approaches, fireflies play,
Bright stars become our cabaret,
With glimmers of nostalgia in our hearts,
The funny moments, where joy imparts.

Unspoken Words at Twilight

At twilight's hush, the air feels thick,
With whispered jokes and a silly trick,
Friends exchange glances, a wink or two,
In this silent dance, there's much to do.

A game of charades takes center stage,
Each gesture wild, no need for age,
Laughter erupts, a symphonic score,
As we lose ourselves in this playful lore.

Hours drift by like funny hats,
Toppling over like clumsy cats,
The stars overhead start to peek,
While we share secrets, laughter's mystique.

In this twilight, where words run free,
The joy shines bright for us to see,
In unspoken moments, sweet and grand,
We treasure the chuckles, hand in hand.

A Journal of Soothing Thoughts

In a nook where whispers dwell,
Pages flip with tales to tell.
A cat naps while dodging a shoe,
As tea spills like morning dew.

Cushions sigh under weighty dreams,
Dancing dust in sunlit beams.
Laughter bursts from creaky seams,
As time unwinds in cozy schemes.

Pencils roll from careless hands,
Naming clouds and their funny bands.
A spider skates on thread so thin,
While a rogue sock dares to spin.

Ticking clocks with quirky chimes,
Mimic music of silly times.
Memory holds a soft embrace,
In this haven, we find our place.

Footsteps on Soft Floors

Socks slide joyfully on the tiles,
Creaking boards play silly styles.
Each step a dance, a giggly prank,
As slippers march, with grace, they flank.

Wobbling cats on tiptoe tread,
Chasing shadows, fun ahead.
A tumble here, a jolly clang,
While laughter echoes in the tang.

Dust bunnies cheer as we parade,
In a march of mischief, unafraid.
Rolls of laughter fill the air,
With each soft footfall, we share.

The world outside may rush and race,
But in these halls, we set the pace.
With every giggle, every jest,
We find our home, we find our best.

Ephemeral Echoes

In the corners where echoes play,
Whispers of laughter drift away.
A yawn and a snore, a dream delayed,
As shadows dance, a serenade.

Bubbles burst with a fizzy cheer,
As time skips like a child here.
A sneeze erupts, a playful shout,
While silly thoughts flit in and out.

Voices meld with the afternoon,
Setting rhymes to a gentle tune.
The chair creaks, a friendly groan,
In this space, we're never alone.

Laughter echoes, light and bright,
Fleeting moments ignite the night.
With every chuckle, a memory grows,
A tapestry of joy that flows.

The Space Between Breaths

In the pauses of our chatter,
Giggles chase like playful patter.
A thoughtful sip, a crooked smile,
Life's little quirks make it worthwhile.

Between the sounds, a silent tease,
A stretch, a yawn, an ill-timed sneeze.
Socks on the line, all mismatched,
Every moment, a puzzle dispatched.

Candles flicker, shadows leap,
Secrets held in swirls and sweep.
Victory dances on chocolate cake,
With every slice, new joy we make.

In the quietest gaps, laughter peeks,
A new adventure in every tweak.
With every room and every sigh,
In the stillness, our spirits fly.

An Interlude of Gentle Breaths

In corners where the socks reside,
A sneezing cat takes things in stride.
The teapot sings, though no one's there,
It whistling tunes, a fragrant air.

A chair that creaks, a floorboard groans,
Beneath the weight of too many bones.
The curtains dance, with flirts of dust,
Each flutter feels like giggles, just.

A clock that tocks is in on the joke,
Pushing its hands while we all choke.
A dog snorts loud, a piglet might,
It's time for tea and a belly fight.

In the midst of all this clatter,
The world outside just doesn't matter.
With each gentle sigh, a chuckle's found,
In the chaos, joy does abound.

Whispers in the Stillness

In the stillness, spoons may clink,
And old chairs creak, as if they think.
A shadow darts, or is it me?
I swear that vase just winked, you see!

Dust bunnies roll like tumbleweeds,
When nobody's around, who heeds?
The scrappy cat, an acrobat,
Flipping through the air—now where's he at?

Gossip flows from mops and brooms,
As if they're sharing the latest glooms.
A cookie jar with secrets stored,
Hides sweets galore, let's be adored!

Each whisper echoes, what a thrill!
A sock's betrayal, oh, what a spill!
Here in the hush, whimsy's a theme,
Life's a silly, silly dream.

Echoes Beneath the Eaves

Under the eaves, the dust motes dance,
A mouse sneezes, seizing his chance.
The old guitar hums a tune,
Echoes of laughter, the afternoon.

A mismatched shoe plays hide and seek,
In a quiet nook, it feels unique.
The shadow of a spider bows,
As critics rave, "Such artsy brows!"

It's here the memories tease and twirl,
Like laundry spun in a dizzy whirl.
The ghost of spilled tea takes a sip,
And rolls with laughter, in a skit.

Beneath the roof, in cozy play,
Whispers of echoes, here they stay.
With giggles softly tucked away,
In this fond space—come join the fray!

Shadows on the Walls

Shadows on the walls, what do they say?
They dance and prance in a funny way.
A broomstick knight, a table queen,
Turning the room into a scene!

The fridge hums tunes of old charm,
As food inside sways, "No alarm!"
Forgotten leftovers start to wave,
A furry friend in the door knave.

With mugs that clink and stir with glee,
Sips of laughter, oh, a jubilee!
The clock rolls its eyes, it's just so late,
As we dream of pie and giraffe fate.

In shadows where memories collide,
The antics bring joy we can't abide.
We chuckle soft, in this quirky place,
In hushed expeditions, we find our grace.

A Song for the Quiet Hour

In the corner, a cat takes a nap,
Dreaming of fish in a sideways flap.
The clock ticks softly, a lullaby's pull,
While dust bunnies dance, oh so wonderful.

A plant hums tunes, or so it seems,
Swaying gently, fulfilling its dreams.
The teapot whistles a high-pitched squeal,
About the secrets it's too shy to reveal.

A chair creaks laughter, stories untold,
While shadows play tag, both daring and bold.
The quiet hour giggles, hiding with glee,
Tickling moments just for you and me.

With laughter soft, the sunlight winks,
Bringing magic to thoughts and drinks.
In this haven, the funny takes flight,
Turning whispers into sheer delight.

Grace of the Unseen

Beneath the sofa, a sock has gone rogue,
Plotting adventures in a dusty prologue.
A remote control, bafflingly shy,
Plays hide and seek, oh my! Oh my!

The window creaks, telling tales from beyond,
While cushions conspire, a secret bond.
The lamp flickers once, with mischief in mind,
Illuminating shadows that are one of a kind.

A spider spins jokes in its silken thread,
While laughter erupts from the book that was read.
The walls have ears and a sense of delight,
Whispering secrets when it's quiet at night.

So here we sit, in this curious space,
With the unseen grace, putting a smile on our face.
In the corners, there lies an unspoken mirth,
A dance of the unseen, for all it's worth.

Traces of Yesterday

Old photos chuckle, their stories a tease,
A family portrait with mismatched ease.
The cat leans in, with a satisfied grin,
Pondering the snacks it may find within.

Yesterday's crumbs leave trails on the floor,
Leading to places we've not been before.
A sock puppet theater plays out a scene,
Of wild adventures, both silly and keen.

The fridge hums softly, a lullaby true,
While leftovers scheme for a grand debut.
And the rug giggles, it's seen it all,
From spilled juice cups to a tumble and fall.

Time fades away like a whimsical tune,
While traces of laughter float up to the moon.
In this space of the past, a joyful refrain,
As moments of yesterday dance in our brain.

Flickers of Hope

In the corner, a light bulb starts to hum,
With a flicker of hope, it goes thrum-thrum-thrum.
The chair leans back, surveying its reign,
While old bricks giggle like they're slightly insane.

The rug's got a story, it's ready to share,
Of feet that have wandered, unaware, unaware!
A capricious breeze blows through the room,
Tickling the curtains, making them bloom.

A cup of cocoa, with a splash of cheer,
Whispers sweet nothings to the comfy sphere.
Cookies once baked play a jig on the plate,
Saying, "Join in, this is going to be great!"

So let's gather close, as the laughter ignites,
Over flickers of hope and cozy delights.
In this whimsical world, where dreams take flight,
Every chuckle unfolds as the day turns to night.

A Sanctuary of Silence

In the corner, a cat takes a nap,
Dreaming of tuna, avoiding a trap.
The clock ticks loudly, but no one can hear,
Except for the mouse, who's buried in cheer.

Tea parties happen, with no guests in sight,
The teapot whistles, what a funny fright!
A vase full of flowers, static and stuck,
They laugh in the sunlight, oh what a luck!

Socks on the ceiling, and hats on the floor,
It's a casual party, come in through the door!
Dust bunnies dance, in a jitterbug spree,
Who knew such chaos could feel so carefree?

In this quiet domain, oddities bloom,
Whispering secrets, amidst all the gloom.
Laughter is hiding, beneath the old sink,
Give a knock on the door, and watch it all wink!

Breath of the Forgotten

Old chairs tell stories, from days of yore,
Unused and dusty, they silently bore.
A stuffed bear nods, from the edge of the shelf,
While mismatched socks play hide-and-seek themselves.

In the cupboard, old cookies crumble away,
They used to be crunchy, now soft as a stray.
Jars full of buttons, and missing a few,
Dare to embrace what once was anew!

An old record spins, with a crack and a squeak,
Dancing shoes whisper, it's laughter they seek.
A harmonica playing the blues on its own,
Melodies linger, like seeds that were sown.

Here's to the moments that flutter and fade,
Caught in a whirlwind, like dreams that we've made.
Tickle me gently with crayons and cheer,
In shadows of laughter, we hold them all dear!

Memories Beneath the Surface

In the basement, there's a treasure trove,
Forgotten relics, where old memories rove.
A trunk filled with hats, and a gown that won't fit,
Each time it's opened, creates quite the wit.

The shelves have a story, or maybe a yarn,
Of bric-a-brac dreams, and a misfit farm.
Slightly askew, the fridge hums its tune,
It's harboring secrets, beneath the blue moon.

A game of charades with puppets galore,
Each gesture a giggle, we'd laugh evermore.
The old rug may warn, as it wobbles along,
That dancing with dust is a very fine song.

In this private place where the oddities dwell,
Let's conjure up laughter with each silly spell.
With whimsy enshrined, in this quaint little space,
The past brings a smile, with its comical grace!

Serenity in the Attic

Up in the attic, where sunlight is shy,
A ghost plays hide-and-seek with a pie.
Cobwebs weave tales, of old summer nights,
When laughter and mischief took hilarious flights.

A suitcase of memories, layered with dust,
Open it gently, it's a must, it's a must!
Jumbled old postcards, with scribbles and jokes,
Reviving the past with all its quirky pokes.

A mirror with smudges, reflects quite the scene,
A dance with a broom, and a hat that's obscene.
The echoes of laughter fit snug in the beams,
Adventures awaken as we drift into dreams.

In this space so serene, where silence is gold,
The laughter within is a treasure to hold.
Tickle the rafters with joy ever true,
In this magical haven, we chase what we knew!

The Canvas of Calm

In a nook with a lamp that hums,
A cat on a chair where nobody comes.
The clock ticks slow, a snail on sun,
And socks dance alone, oh what fun!

With tea that spills, and giggles that flow,
A window whispers, 'What's outside? Who knows?'
The dust bunnies waltz, on the floor they twirl,
In this silly shanty, where chaos can swirl.

Chairs wobble gently, as if they might sing,
While spoons have debates about who's the best bling.
A mirror reflects a mischievous grin,
As I squeegee my thoughts, let the laughter begin!

So here's to the moments, serene yet bizarre,
Where silence is gold, and the heart goes far.
In corners of calm, let mischief abound,
As joy flickers softly, with no one around.

Sonnet of the Unsung

In a room where the slippers have parties at night,
A pillow confesses the jokes that ignite.
The fridge hums a tune that's all out of tune,
While the broom taps the beat, for a soliloquy tune.

A chair plays the jester, cracked and amused,
While the curtains giggle, brightly bemused.
The dust motes pirouette in a ray's golden glow,
And the clock grins wide, with nowhere to go.

Socks on the floor hold a mock ball, I swear,
While the table debates with a skip of a chair.
The walls hold their breath, listening in glee,
As the house chuckles gently, alive like a bee.

With laughter in whispers, and giggles unheard,
This sanctuary's secrets, oh how they've stirred!
In the quiet unseen, where joy finds its song,
We dance with the moments, all giggly and strong.

A Reverie Wrapped in Stillness

Beneath the calm ceiling, a spider weaves dreams,
Where echoes of laughter float softly in streams.
A sock, mismatched, is the room's finest guest,
As it chats with the lamp post, feeling quite blessed.

Between the four walls, the air's full of cheer,
With whispers of things that are often unclear.
The chair with the squeak plays the part of the clown,
While the coat on the hook cracks a smile, not a frown.

Afternoons linger like a lazy parade,
As the teapot spills tales with no need for a raid.
A cushion, quite comfy, has stories to share,
While the rogue little rug dreams without a care.

So here in the hush, where delight does not cease,
We find joy in the stillness, a bubbling peace.
In the corners of time, where the silly takes flight,
We waltz through the moments, wrapped gently in light.

Comfort in the Unheard

In whispers of corners where shadows are loud,
The couch has opinions that come wrapped in a cloud.
The carpet's a storyteller, ink sourced from dust,
While the plants roll their leaves in a dance of pure trust.

A teapot brews tales of escapes far and wide,
While spoons natter softly, with pride on their side.
A window grins wide as the breeze gives a shout,
While the clock spins round, 'What's this all about?'

The fridge holds its secrets, a friend in the night,
While the mop tries to tango, oh what a sight!
A chair creaks in rhythm to the beats of the hour,
Embracing the chaos with whimsical power.

Here's to the comfort we find in the still,
Where chuckles and whispers create all the thrill.
In a haven so odd, yet wonderfully clear,
We whisper the moments, and laugh without fear.

Dance of Dust Motes

In sunlight beams they flit and sway,
With tiny moves that steal the day.
They jig and jive, a lively crew,
While I just sneeze, 'Achoo! Achoo!'

They swirl and twirl in air so light,
A daily show, both strange and bright.
My broom stands still, it seems to pout,
As dust balls dance and flitter out.

Their grand ballet makes me want to clap,
Yet they are gone, just like a nap.
I laugh and grin, what a grand sight,
These motes find joy in pure delight!

But then I sneeze; the curtain falls,
And silence reigns within these walls.
Oh, dust, you jesters of the air,
Please come back soon, I've time to spare!

In the Presence of Solace

A chair sits nice, it winks at me,
With built-in charms for full esprit.
It creaks and groans, it knows my name,
In this sweet place, I find my fame.

The cat sprawls wide, a furry queen,
In shadows deep, she's rarely seen.
She purrs and snores, I let out a chuckle,
As she dreams dreams of mice and snuggle.

The clocks tick on, a comedic tease,
While I lounge here, oh such ease!
A snack or two, my laughter grows,
As crumbs fall down, igniting shows.

This quiet bliss, at times so loud,
Where solitude wears a cozy shroud.
I find my joy in simple things,
As laughter blooms, my heart it sings!

The Auras of Rest

In peaceful realms of soft, warm light,
I chase my dreams till edge of night.
Beneath the blankets, I spin and roll,
A cozy cocoon, my funny soul.

The window creaks, a ghostly sigh,
As I pretend to be a spy.
I giggle at shadows on the wall,
And whisper secrets like it's a ball!

Those dusty books wear wisdom's crown,
But honestly, they just bring me down!
I pick one up, but alas, oh dear,
The plot is dull; I shed a tear.

Yet still I grin, for dreams collide,
With oddball thoughts I cannot hide.
In quiet corners, laughter blooms,
As sleepy smiles light up the rooms!

Whispered Thoughts at Midnight

At midnight's hour, ideas sprout,
Like mushrooms growing all about.
A lightbulb flickers in my head,
I laugh so hard, it wakes the dead!

The shadowy walls play hide and seek,
While thoughts dance wildly, cheek to cheek.
I scribble tales, a silly quest,
As midnight snack seems like a jest.

A cup of tea, it spills with grace,
As I try hard to pick up pace.
What fun it is, in this delight,
To chase the whims of blissful night!

While giggles slip through midnight's veil,
And hush the whispers, light as a sail.
I'd trade it all for one more hour,
In quiet joys, I find my power!

www.ingramcontent.com/pod-product-compliance
Lightning Source LLC
Chambersburg PA
CBHW062112280426
43661CB00086B/498